THE ANATOMY OF A COMEBACK

CARL GOULD
&
CHUCK GOETSCHEL

TABLE OF CONTENTS

Foreword 1

Introduction 5

CHAPTER ONE: I Knew the Dog Was Going to Die 8

CHAPTER TWO: From Mowing Lawns to Coaching CEOs.. 22

Chapter THREE: Break In 30

Chapter FOUR: Breakthrough 47

Chapter FIVE: Break Out....................................... 63

Chapter SIX: Break Away 94

Epilogue 117

THE ANATOMY OF A COMEBACK

FOREWORD

"One does not see anything until one sees its beauty." —Oscar Wilde

As we grow businesses and lives, the negative perspectives, articles, blogs, and words of others too frequently influence us. However, sometimes we're blessed with a new set of eyes. It allows us to look at situations or challenges from a fresh perspective that perhaps we hadn't yet considered.

Recently my four-year-old sat on a stool near the bathroom sink watching me shave. He asked important questions like: "why don't I need to do that, Daddy?" and "why don't baseball players wear shorts?" Then he said, "Daddy, your skin is so ridgy, bumpy and red."

He paused for a few seconds, tracing one of the scars with his index finger, and added, "but I really like it."

You see, as a child I was burned on 100% of my body, spent months in hospital and years in therapy. It took me 20 years to see any beauty in those scars. Even today, when I am honest about it, there are moments when I have a very difficult time seeing good in them. There are times when I host the pity parties or wish they weren't there or feel less-than-perfect.

And he "really likes it?"

What so many view as negative, a little boy (innocent, blinded to prejudice, open to real beauty) sees the scars – not for the marks of imperfection others see – but for the badge of beauty and courage which they are.

My friends, the unavoidable consequence of life is that we all get burned; we all have scars. They appear physically, internally, relationally, financially and professionally. Mistakes are made, wounds open, and scars appear. We rarely acknowledge their existence, rarely acknowledge their lessons, and rarely acknowledge the blessings of those events.

I've discovered that it is the scars that propel us forward in life. They lead to compassion, the growth of a network, the expansion of possibility, the awakening of humility, the desire for a stronger purpose, the reaffirmation of beliefs, and the foundation of resilience. These are the keys to a successful business. These are the keys to a successful life.

Every success I've been fortunate enough to enjoy in life was born through tragic, scarring experiences, and a long, painful battle forward. My growth spiritually is the result of realizing life is about a cause and purpose much more than myself. My growth relationally is the result of an early awareness of the sacred value of others and the need to meet them compassionately. And my growth in business, at Rising Above, is the result of never giving into fear and always racing forward on fire with passion, purpose and the truth that the best is yet to come.

When you embrace the truth that mistakes, missteps, brokenness, challenges, and seeming defeat serve as the foundation for your greatest success, you'll be able to look in your mirror each day with new eyes, acknowledging your scars, saying, "they might be ridgy, bumpy and red……but I really like them!"

This book will help you come back to the realization that all of the scars, all of the burns and all of the challenges are making you stronger and more resilient than ever. Enjoy Chuck's Comeback story, and Carl's "play-by-play" analysis.

Yours in comeback,

John O'Leary
www.RisingAbove.com

INTRODUCTION

Meet Dan. He was an upper level manager in the customer service department of a large corporation for 11 years, and he has just been laid off. Worse yet, when he started looking for a new job, he found that countless companies were outsourcing their entire customer service departments overseas. The jobs he was qualified for no longer existed.

Now meet Terry. She started her own business 18 months ago with a line of credit on the home that she and her husband have owned for 10 years. They knew the first few years would be tight, but they were confident that the equity in their home could sustain them until her venture began returning a reliable profit. There was only one problem: the value of their home fell so sharply during the housing bust that the bank decreased their line of credit by 90%, even though they had never missed a payment.

Dan and Terry represent the millions of Americans today who are out of work, out of credit, or simply out of luck. In most cases, they were born into relatively favorable circumstances, worked hard and just when their dreams seemed within reach, everything came crashing down around them.

A few decades ago, Americans were more accustomed to an economy that appeared to have seasons. After the abundance of an autumn harvest, trees would shed leaves and companies would shed jobs. Such changes were expected and prepared for. Unfortunately, many in this particular generation are ill-equipped to navigate the current winter.

Countless of individuals feel as though they are lost in a hostile land without a map. And that feeling often elicits one of two reactions: denial or despair. Those in denial are vulnerable to get-rich-quick schemes, refusing to accept the reality of their current situation, and assuming that there must be some painless path to better times. Those in despair will make irrational choices rooted in hopelessness and fear.

But there is another way to react when you've been

knocked down. I know: I went from earning a high six-figure salary to being unable to afford an apartment, but I came back stronger than ever. I will share the details of my story, as will my co-author, Carl, but for now, suffice it to say that we both know a thing or two about being knocked down. This book—drawing on our experiences and those of countless others we've coached—explains how to face the reality of your knock-down, and orchestrate your Comeback.

If you or a loved one is in a place where life feels like it's happening *to* you, this book will show you how to take back the reins. If you feel defined by your problems and your struggles, this book will teach you how to be defined by the steps you take to overcome them. This book is a story: the story of my Comeback and, ultimately, the story of yours.

CHAPTER ONE: I KNEW THE DOG WAS GOING TO DIE

"I'm sorry sir, but you don't qualify." The woman's voice was crisp and firm.

"Wait a minute," I protested in disbelief. "Are you telling me that I don't qualify to adopt a dog that you just found last night on the side of the freeway?"

"Yes, sir. That's exactly what I'm saying."

I couldn't believe my ears. Not too long ago, I was being flown by private jet to speak in front of tens of thousands of people. Now an animal shelter was telling me that they would sooner euthanize this little black Labrador than let me take it home.

THE ANATOMY OF A COMEBACK

I have been a dog lover almost as long as I can remember, having found them to be some of nature's deepest wells of unconditional love. After a mere thirty minutes at the shelter, this little Lab and I had already bonded. He growled warmly as I scratched him behind his ears and under his jaw, and I could already picture myself throwing the Frisbee with him in the park, or reading on the couch at night with him at my feet.

The woman behind the counter was avoiding my gaze, but I knew I had no hope of talking her out of her decision. I took one last look into the shining dark eyes of that innocent pup, and I felt my heart breaking. All I could think of was the fact that he would probably be dead within the month.

That dog represented my last hope for a friend, for someone or something to save me from the downward spiral that had overtaken every waking hour of my life. As I thought about his inevitable death, I could not help but think that we were sharing the same fate: I was physically alive, but everything I had loved and worked for my entire life had been taken away.

For years, I had enjoyed the freedom and luxury of a multimillionaire with a beautiful wife and, over time, two young children. An athlete since childhood, I had been in tremendous physical shape and full of energy.

I owned spectacular homes, travelled all over the world and drove around town in variety of luxury cars.

Then in a flash, it was gone.

I lost my business, money, family and possessions in what felt like an instant.

My net worth seemed to reverse overnight, and I was completely alone. I stopped eating. I had no energy. I became depressed and unable to function. My last hope for love and companionship was adopting a stray dog. And now I couldn't even do that.

As I walked several blocks home, I began to feel an overwhelming ache in the very core of my soul. I have fallen to the bottom, I thought.

I paused before my front door. The weather was pleasant enough, but I felt inexplicably chilly. As I fished around in my pocket for my keys, I began to wonder if this was really the end for me. I would never have taken my own life, but I began to imagine that I might simply cease to exist. Everything I had lived for was gone, seemingly forever.

THE ANATOMY OF A COMEBACK

What I know now, but didn't know then, was that that moment was not the end for me. It was the beginning of my Comeback.

WHAT HAPPENED?

The loss of everything that was important in my life—my family, my business, my investments and my influence—all came crashing down at once. It was the perfect storm for disaster between a challenged marriage, a dramatic change in business, and a plummeting economy.

It began with the unfortunate demise of my first marriage. As I boarded a flight home from a meeting, I received a text from my wife: "Don't bother coming home. I've moved you out."

Although after 12 years together we had been experiencing some extreme challenges in our marriage, and despite my own disrespectful behavior, this came as a complete shock to me. My own parents, at the time of writing, have been married over 50 years. My grandparents, both of whom lived to be nearly 100, were married for 74 years. I never dreamed on my darkest day that I would ever get divorced.

Then, my business took an unbelievable turn. Without inviting yet another lawsuit, I will explain the situation as simply as I possibly can. I had been part of a large direct sales corporation for many years. I had risen to the very highest ranks with thousands of individuals under my leadership.

One June morning, I was summoned into a large board meeting with other top leaders. We went through the usual preliminary business, listening to reports from each division. Then one of the executives began to speak.

"As most of you know by now," he began, "we've decided to move forward with a major transformation during the upcoming quarters." My ears perked up. Was he announcing what I thought? As he continued his explanation, I got a sick feeling in my stomach— they were discussing the very change they had vowed, in my opinion, would never happen.

I listened some more, hoping against hope that I was misunderstanding them. But the more he talked, the clearer it became. What's more, everyone quickly realized the advisory board had no ability to stop the 180 degree turn the company was making, let alone the thousands of people who stood to have their personal financial situations ruined.

Even by the company's own analysis, it would be a devastating blow to the thousands of people I oversaw.

I suggested various alternative solutions, including some exit options for the people, but nothing I proposed was even remotely considered. Repeatedly, I was told, "It's the cost of doing business."

Over the next few days, the executives reminded me that if I would simply get behind the program and go back and "spin it to the people," then I was already in line for a new $500,000 bonus.

"That's not a bonus, it's a bribe," I said, horrified.

I pondered my next step—after all, they were going to do what they were going to do with or without my blessing. Still, I knew in my heart I could never affirm their decision. In my opinion, they were breaking their word and ruining thousands of people's finances. It would happen no matter what I did, but I simply couldn't support it.

NOW WHAT?

I tendered my letter of resignation, along with my reasons for leaving. I didn't exactly have a plan, but I assumed I could look for a contract with a similar company, perhaps expand some of my other business dealings, and liquidate some of my real estate holdings in the meantime. We might have to tighten the belt a little for a while, but I was sure everything was going to be okay.

But everything was far from okay.

I had always assumed that the life we were leading was secure, but I soon learned it was a house of cards just waiting to tumble down. Technically, we could afford all our homes and cars, but all our extra money was tied up in long term business ventures and real estate. As much as I put money in several different places, I only had one reliable source of income, and that was the company I had just left. It would be years before I could expect my other ventures to bear significant fruit.

Then, as luck would have it, the real estate market went south. The holdings I was hoping to liquidate were more or less frozen, sitting on the market for months, losing value by the minute. I know that millions of other Americans experienced exactly the same as I did, seeing their net-worth collapse almost overnight. Regardless of the path you took to get there, it is a terrible feeling when it happens.

Next, I learned that my former company wasn't done with me yet. Because my departure made their bad public relations situation even worse, they began to sue me and a handful of others. While, in my opinion, they had no real grounds to repeatedly bring me to court, the lawsuits served several purposes: First, they cast doubt on my character. If you are being sued for anything, no matter how ridiculous, it will cause people to think twice before trusting you. Second, the pending litigation prevented me from speaking publicly about what had happened. And third, as anyone who has ever been sued knows, it was a highly effective form of harassment—it cost me time, money and precious energy to answer the lawsuits.

The litigation was ongoing over an extended period of time. They took and scanned the computers from my home, and sent me around the country: as one suit completed, they'd file another—same suit, new state. The lead attorney once told me, "Chuck, for me this is job security. We can do this forever, until you can't."

Next my soon-to-be-ex wife sought permission to move away with our children. The threat made me physically ill. I had braced myself for the worst when she announced that she had moved me out of the house, but the thought of not seeing my two young boys again on a regular basis was more than I could bear.

To pour gasoline on the fire, someone chose this moment to steal my identity and run up an account of ten thousand dollars in materials from Home Depot. I remember thinking that if I was trying to sell a screenplay of my life at that time, Hollywood producers would have rejected it for being "over the top."

Once all of these events were in motion, it was only a matter of time before the houses were foreclosed on, property seized, cars repossessed and every other unpleasant thing you can imagine happened. Every phone call was from a bill collector. Every piece of mail was a subpoena for the custody hearing, another lawsuit from my company, or Home Depot grinding what was left of my credit into the dirt. Soon, it was all I could do to get out of bed.

Then I got rejected when I tried to adopt a stray dog.

THE TURNING POINT

The day I was denied the dog, I felt as if I had reached out for a comforting hug and been punched in the gut instead. But just as a sucker-punch will sometimes trigger the fight in the weariest of men, the experience was a wake-up call. For weeks, I had been walking around in a daze, passively accepting what life had thrown at me, unable to string two coherent thoughts together to plan a response. I was no longer living my life; life was inflicting itself on me.

It was only when I couldn't adopt that dog—when I realized that a charitable organization had decided that a stray dog was better off dead than in my care—that I decided that I had had enough. I regret that it took all of these things to bring me to this place, but

---

I finally did what so many desperate souls do: I fell to my knees.

I cannot tell you exactly what did it—whether it was calling out to my Creator and Savior, humbling myself to realize that I couldn't fix this on my own, or connecting with His transcendent purpose that is higher than myself—but I rose from my knees with renewed strength.

A NEW DAY

We live in an era that glorifies victimhood. And truly, given the challenges we all face at times, it can be very tempting to focus on the ways in which others have wronged us. And most people don't have to look far: we can all find legitimate disappointments in our relationships and at work, and sometimes we can even find grave injustices. Yet the strength I found that day came not in denying what had been done to me, but in rejecting the *role* of the victim. No longer was I going to sit back and watch these terrible things happen to me. I was going to take charge.

To my shock, the most empowering thing I did was to find every possible way to take responsibility for the situation I was in.

I had arrived here first and foremost because of a decision I voluntarily made: I didn't have to walk away from my multi-million dollar business, but I did, and I decided, even in that horrible situation, that I would do it again. But what *else* could I take responsibility for?

To answer that question, I had to go back to years of choices and patterns of behavior that had brought me to the place where that one decision could bring my entire life crashing down around me. First, I recognized that I had put all my financial eggs in one basket. Sure,

THE ANATOMY OF A COMEBACK

I had investments, but ultimately, 95% of my income came from one contract. I had real estate and private equity investments, but not nearly enough cash on hand in savings to protect myself and my family in case of an emergency.

Then there was my marriage: I had always loved my wife, but I realized that I had taken her for granted. I was so focused on work that I failed to give my time and attention to her as much as I should have. I naively thought my financial rewards were enough to bless our marriage. And, when she felt hurt and acted out, I thought that I was the one being wronged. I had mistakenly taken the examples of long, successful marriages in my own family to mean that my wife would be there for me—supporting and affirming me—even while I paid attention to other things. Ironically, I learned the most about relationships in those ensuing months when I was almost entirely alone. I'll share more about those lessons in the chapters that follow.

Ultimately, I learned that when you play the role of the victim, you have to wait for someone else to rescue you. You're trapped with no way out; you have no power to make your situation better. Yet when you take responsibility, no matter how painful or unfair it seems, all of a sudden you are in control. You can change your own decisions, even if you cannot change the decisions of others.

I began to slowly, painfully correct the problems that I detected during this process of self-examination and soul searching. I stopped taking my relationships for granted. It was too late for my marriage, but I threw myself into my relationship with my boys, and drew inspiration from my parents and the friends that had always believed in me. I appreciated their love and support so much more than I ever had when circumstances were favorable, and I vowed to appreciate them for the rest of my life. I was coming back.

Miraculously, long before I was secure again financially, I met a wonderful woman named Wendy. She loved me enough to marry me, even in my rather vulnerable state. And she, along with her sweet, autistic son, traveled through this difficult time with me. More than once she found herself in the checkout line at the grocery store with a declined debit card. She battled humiliation and fear, and observed every step of my Comeback. This journey became her story as well.

I'm grateful to report that life has only got better and better. Mercifully, my boys remained nearby, and we are with them regularly. Wendy gave birth to our daughter just 14 months after our wedding. In time, my new company grew, and prospered while I personally became a better version of myself.

What's more, I appreciate what I have so much more than I did before. I am grateful to God for His unconditional love and omnipotent guidance. I am aware of each moment, each blessing, each memory, rather than brushing past them to pay attention to other things that really don't matter. I'm extremely grateful.

And yes, I now have a dog.

CHAPTER TWO:
FROM MOWING LAWNS TO COACHING CEOS

Carl's story: Growing up in a large family is great. There's always someone to play basketball or football with you, someone to help you with homework, someone to beat up on, and someone to beat up on you. You may have to fight over the last slice of pot roast, but you will never be bored. As one of ten kids, I experienced these blessings every day of my childhood.

And it really was a good childhood. Looking back on it, it seemed like it was one big ongoing family reunion. The prevailing attitude seemed to be "Work hard, play hard." Parents, grandparents, aunts and uncles all worked their tails off at their jobs, but when the came time to relax, the food was devoured and the beer kegs were drained. I can't think of a single family member who didn't know how to live it up.

But we were also go-getters. Both my parents were entrepreneurs, Dad running an IT consulting firm and Mom owning one of the earliest direct marketing companies. My four brothers and I all became business owners as teenagers—in everything from distribution to contracting—and two of my five sisters opted for entrepreneurial careers as well. So business was in the blood!

I launched my first landscaping company at seventeen. I loved being outside, and I found it very rewarding to transform a property in a very short time. Soon, I had to hire others, and we expanded into lawn maintenance and other services.

Five years later, I sustained a knee injury and sold the company. I could no longer do the work myself, and I hadn't yet learned how to delegate. So I started a general contracting and real estate development company. It took me a while to get the hang of a new industry, but after a couple of years, that business was thriving as well.

There was a problem, though. I was doing fine financially, but I had almost no free time. If you are a business owner, you may be able to identify with me. I was swamped; no matter how much I got done during those "normal" working hours between 9:00 and 5:00, there was always more to do. In short, I wasn't running my business: it was running me.

I knew I was doing what I loved, but I also knew I needed help to do it the right way. So I hired a business advisor to help me structure my company in a way that would allow me to "fire myself" from some of the extra tasks I didn't need to be doing. That process taught me the ins and outs of guiding a company to its full maturity: the stage where I, as the owner, was only doing what I wanted to do.

But something else was going on as well.

The more successful I became, the more people gravitate to me for advice.

These conversations soon became regular sessions, and before I knew it, I was a part time life coach. I was helping people come back from tough times, and helping others simply get better. What's more, I loved it! I really enjoyed working with people to help them set goals, create a plan, and then execute that plan. Some days, I almost felt that I was running my contracting business in order to support my coaching addiction.

As I continued to fire myself from various jobs in my contracting company, I found myself with more and more free time. I was able to successfully train my employees and vendors, and discovered that more and more work was getting done without me. Any entrepreneur can understand how wonderful that experience is. I started feeling less self-employed and more like a CEO!

About eight years after I first hired my business consultant, I launched my own international consulting agency. I began working with decision makers in all types of organizations. It was tremendously rewarding to combine my coaching skills with my experiences as a business owner and CEO. My clients' businesses grew. and so did mine.

During this process,

I discovered an ironic truth: greater success can lead to greater isolation.

I now found myself counseling many of the people I might have normally gone to for advice myself. Realizing I lacked a professional support system, I found a business owners' group where I could share my experiences with other like-minded people, and hear about theirs as well. It was entrepreneurs helping entrepreneurs, and it was a perfect fit for me. This group not only understood where I was coming from, they were also performing at a level similar to mine, if not higher. They not only listened, but also provided extremely helpful feedback.

I found the experiences and achievements of these men and women extremely inspiring, and I felt a renewed sense of energy about my business and my personal growth. I learned firsthand the important role that your peer group plays in your success. I wanted to be around people that motivated me to stay on track, as well as to do, and to be, more.

THE ANATOMY OF A COMEBACK

MY COMEBACK

At this point, you may be wondering what I know about making a Comeback. Well, my crisis didn't come from an unexpected financial loss, but from a personal one. When I was 23 years old, I received a phone call from the police. My brother Jon, after a weekend of golf and partying, failed to negotiate a turn on a windy country road while driving home. After the crash, a dog alerted a nearby homeowner to Jon's presence, and the man immediately called 911. Unfortunately, Jon's neck was broken and he died before the ambulance got there.

I had dealt with death before, and even deaths I now consider premature. But losing my brother shocked me beyond belief. I had lost my hero and my best friend, which was more than I could process. Nothing had prepared me for that level of emotional torment.

Although my business was doing well at the time, when Jon died I lost my drive to do anything. I sank into despair and then a deep depression. It's crazy to think about hitting rock bottom before you're 25, but there I was. I was financially, physically and emotionally devastated. It just didn't seem fair.

After nearly a year of feeling about as low as a person can feel, I hit some sort of critical mass. I finally became fed up with my situation: I became sick and tired of being sick and tired. The change was triggered when I realized that I was doing nothing to honor my brother's memory by living my life so pitifully. I needed to make a change. I didn't know what I was going to do, or how I was going to do it, but I was finally ready to do whatever it took.

For me, the catalyst for turning my life around at a relatively young age was taking charge of my physical health. Chuck and I will share more details in the chapter that follows, but I learned in my Comeback experience that once you've figured out how to overcome a crisis, the process and skills involved can be applied to any situation. Coming back from a lifelong allergy problem and poor health taught me how to implement positive and consistent changes to the way I ate and exercised. Then I was able to apply those same principles to the way I ran my business.

What's more, you don't need to wait for a crisis or setback in order to apply these principles. I have helped countless clients apply these principles to their own lives and businesses in order to operate at peak performance. Sometimes you just need a Comeback from mediocrity, not disaster!

For me, mediocrity was a disaster: not because my life was a mess, but because I knew I was capable of so much more.

Jon's final gift to me was a wake-up call to make the most of my life. I think of him every day, and I work to make him proud by answering that call.

CHAPTER THREE: BREAK IN

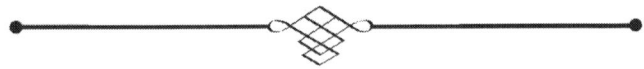

"Sometimes I can't tell at all what's going on in that head of yours."

Renee Zellweger's plea to Tom Cruise in the 1996 movie *Jerry McGuire* was a familiar refrain for many couples. Like so many wives, she longed to "Break In" to her husband's thoughts and motivations: to understand what made him tick. But like many men, Tom Cruise's character found it easier to live his life on the surface and ignore the inner workings of his soul.

Superficial living seems to work pretty well until you hit a crisis. Disaster has a way of forcing you to take inventory. Like a kidnapping victim thrown in the trunk of a car and dumped by the side of the road, you are left to wonder, "Where am I, and how did I get here?"

In order to orchestrate your Comeback, you must look beneath the surface and confront the reality of your situation and how you got there. You must face your habits, thoughts and patterns of decision-making. You must "Break In" to your own head, your own heart, and deal honestly with what you find there. Chuck will explain.

FACING THE FACTS

The Break In is, in many ways, the most painful part of the Comeback process. I was suffering for a very long time before I was willing to Break In; it took a rejection for a dog adoption to motivate me enough to face the reality of where I was in life. For Carl, it took the death of his brother. Many people who are facing tough times have similar reservations: they want to cling to the delusion that everything is fine until the last possible moment. In fact, they will make many poor choices just to prolong the fantasy that everything is okay.

I remember Carl telling me of an acquaintance of his, "Tammy," who was facing an impending eviction from her apartment. She and her husband had been living far beyond their means for many years. Their car had already been repossessed, and they had maxed out several credit cards. Her husband was a salesman working on commission, so his income varied month to month. Each time they made a risky decision—financing some furniture for their daughter's bedroom, putting some clothing on the credit card, taking that much-needed vacation—they hoped that his income would rise the following month to make up for it. After a while, the bills caught up with them.

Even when faced with an eviction notice, Tammy refused to pack. She held out hope that something would happen at the eleventh hour to allow them to stay. Only on the day before the sheriff would have come to forcibly remove them did she finally accept the reality of their situation. They put their belongings into storage, moved in with friends, and were finally forced to take stock of their lives. They finally Broke In.

When I lost my business, I was also hit with six figures in alimony payments. I had astronomical mortgages on multiple properties, and of course all the associated expenses, including utilities, maintenance and so on. Add to that all my legal expenses from both my work and personal life, and I was running well in excess of $20,000 in the hole each month. It was not a pretty picture.

Somehow, I managed to stay in denial for quite some time. I kept thinking to myself, "I just need to get through this lawsuit, or sell a property, or cash out these private placement stocks." As a result, I never even attempted to get my alimony payments adjusted, or to do anything else that would have made my situation a little more bearable.

This sounds very basic, but until you face your true current position, you will never be able to make real progress towards your intended target. If you want to drive to Chicago, you can't start driving until you know exactly where you are. In fact someone starting all the way in Los Angeles will get there before someone starting in Indianapolis if the guy in LA knows the precise address of the destination and the other person has only a vague idea of his current location. The sooner you face the facts— the total amount of your debts, the amount you actually spend every month, your true income—the sooner you will be on the road to your Comeback.

HOW DID I GET HERE?

Once I faced the reality of my true situation, I had to analyze the decisions that had brought me to that place. I had to do this for every area of my life, but particularly my finances. This was a painful process, but it was also extremely empowering.

Let me explain: every situation like mine results from a combination of decisions and circumstances. It is very tempting to focus on the role that circumstances have played in the difficulties we face, feeling sorry for ourselves and lamenting the unfairness of life. In my case, I could have focused on the real estate market crash and my company's behavior, instead of my own decision to spend and invest my money in particular ways. This would have been an easy way to avoid taking responsibility for the role I had played in my own misery.

Now I want to be clear that some crises are truly beyond people's control: natural disasters, plane crashes, and many other tragedies strike innocent people who have done nothing to bring such events upon themselves. In such cases, it is fair to simply ask yourself, "Where am I, and where do I go from here?" But in a situation like mine—and I would venture to say in most crises of a financial nature—my focus on the aspects that were beyond my control was keeping me trapped.

You see, when we ignore the role our decisions play in bringing about our crisis, we make ourselves passive victims.

The more I told myself that there was little or nothing I could have done to avoid what had happened to me, the more I was subconsciously telling myself that there was nothing I could do to come back from it.

Passive victims can't rescue themselves: they have to wait for a hero to ride in on a white horse, or for circumstances to magically change.

But after the failed dog adoption, I began to look honestly at the decisions I had made which had left me so vulnerable to the circumstances that had overtaken me. Before my world crashed around me, nothing about the outward appearances of my financial situation would have raised a red flag. But when I really

Broke In, I realized I was using money in a way that wasn't healthy.

When I began to take stock of my process for making financial decisions, I recalled a time I was driving to a business appointment, when the guy I was meeting called me and cancelled. I was so frustrated! I hung up my phone and, still driving, I noticed a Porsche dealership to my left. I got off at the next exit and turned around. That night I drove home in a brand new black-on-black convertible Porsche Carrera complete with carbon fiber trim. Why? Because it made me feel better. There were definitely times I was using money to soothe negative emotions, rather than confronting those feelings head on.

I also had to confront the fact that I had spent money as if my current level of income was guaranteed into the foreseeable future. The same was true of millions of Americans who got burned in any of the booms and busts of the past several decades. Investors in technology stocks assumed they would only go up in value. Investors in real estate assumed that housing prices would continue to rise forever. This is like measuring the temperature every day from

June to July and assuming that, based on that information, you'll never need to buy a coat.

Just as you can't evaluate your wardrobe needs based on summer temperatures alone, you can't determine your financial needs based only on good times. Part of being financially responsible is being prepared for seasons like the one I endured. So as I "Broke In" to discover where I was and how I got there, I realized that a huge part of my problem was failing to prepare for a season of lack.

But there were other factors—character qualities and habits that were deeply ingrained—which had been instrumental in getting me into the terrible place I was. And in order to ensure I could move forward, I had to ask myself more painful questions.

CHECK YOUR BLIND SPOT

Edward G. Bulwer Lytton famously said, "The easiest person to deceive is one's self." The Hebrew prophet Jeremiah lamented similarly, "The heart is deceitful above all things…Who can understand it?" All of us are skilled at deceiving ourselves when we want to.

To orchestrate a Comeback, we have to Break In past that self-deception and take an honest look at our strengths, weaknesses and blind spots.

Our greatest strengths can also be our greatest weaknesses. If we are not careful, boldness can become recklessness. We've all heard the saying, nothing ventured, nothing gained. And it is true that anything worthwhile in life involves a degree of risk. However, there are is an optimal amount of risk in life, just as there is an optimal amount of salt in your food. Too little leaves it bland and too much over a long enough period of time might kill you. Carl's natural sense of adventure and willingness to take risks had become more than a weakness: it had become a blind spot. He was no longer able to see how unreasonable the risks were that he took, because he was so drawn to the thrill they provided.

I had a great ability to focus on my work, but often at the expense of neglecting my family. I was so accustomed to being focused on productivity, that I was unable to see how my most important relationship was slipping away from me.

What about you? What are your strengths—the things that seem to come naturally or that you do exceptionally well? Are there ways these strengths have become weaknesses or even blind spots for you? Perhaps you are a great visionary who has difficulty focusing on details. On the other hand you might be great at completing daily tasks, but you haven't yet established long term goals for yourself. Whatever your situation, it is essential to begin your Comeback with an honest and thorough self-evaluation.

THE STORIES WE TELL OURSELVES

Life is a story.

Over the centuries, academics and philosophers have offered numerous theories on how we understand ourselves. Most recently, professors like Dan P. McAdams of Northwestern University are convinced that the life stories we construct for ourselves play a central role in our identity and relationships. These stories are begun in childhood and solidified in adolescence. For the rest of our lives, we fit our experiences into what we see as the stories of our lives.

This is perhaps not quite as new as it might sound. After all, when God told the Israelites to celebrate Passover, He was commanding them to repeat the story of the Exodus to remind them who they were. In the centuries that followed, they would have many ups and downs: they would enjoy tremendous political and military dominance under King David, only to be scattered among the nations. Yet through all this, their identity was strengthened by the story they repeated each year during the celebration of Passover.

When I lost everything, I began to find my identity in the tragedy of my story. I was to be pitied. My life was so sad it was almost comic. I became surprisingly comfortable with my role in the story as the victim, and subconsciously I began to expect everything to go poorly for me.

Hardly a week went by when I didn't hear someone tell me that my best days were behind me and that I should just settle for whatever came my way. "You're confusing your dreams with your fantasies, Chuck," I was told. "You were lucky once. Don't expect lightning to strike again." That became the recurring storyline of my life, silently influencing not only my mood and my outlook on life, but also the way I made decisions.

THE ANATOMY OF A COMEBACK

When you've been successful financially, it's easy to feel that losing your job or losing your business causes you to lose your identity.

When we don't know ourselves well enough, it becomes easier to accept what others say we are.

I was wandering around in this terrible state for quite some time, but finally realized I couldn't do it any longer. I realized that I was so used to telling my tragic story to the hundreds, possibly thousands of people who inquired from around the world, that I had lulled myself into being so much less than I was capable of. And I finally realized that being less than God created me to be was wrong.

When I began to Break In, I recognized how destructive this narrative was to me, and I determined to change it. I was no longer the victim, and my Comeback had nothing to do with the luck of lightening striking again, but rather, after some adjustments, it was about setting myself on fire.

What characterizes the defining story of your life? Are you the hero or the victim? The Israelites' story was one of deliverance and redemption. The outcome of their story did not rest on their perfection, but on their awareness of their imperfections. What about you? Is the story that defines your life one of tragedy or triumph?

WATCHING RERUNS

Often, our lives follow patterns that are easy for others to see, even if we can't seem to recognize them ourselves. In order to Break In, we must have the courage and clarity to identify these patterns. In my own life, I was in a pattern of spending money on outward luxuries.

We are often tempted to look solely at financial decisions—such as the amount we spend, the job we take or the business we start—when looking for financial mistakes. But almost any mistake in life can affect our finances negatively. For example, the decision to divorce is not primarily a financial one, but it can have devastating financial effects. A habit like smoking can end up costing thousands both to support, and in damage to your health.

THE ANATOMY OF A COMEBACK

Is there a bad episode in your life that keeps repeating itself? It could be a mistake you keep promising yourself you'll never repeat, or a habit you just can't seem to break. It could be a relationship that's doing you more harm than good.

Whatever the bad "rerun" is in your life, identifying it is the first step towards changing it.

CARL'S BREAK IN

Although my Comeback involved my entire life, my Break In was directly related to my physical health. My family, as I mentioned, knew how to live it up. My first clue that there was a little more to life than an ongoing party came when I was six years old. I had a very special relationship with the grandfather after whom I was named. I remember riding around with him in the taxi service he owned, being introduced with pride as his namesake. Shortly after my sixth birthday, he became ill and died. It was sad and surreal. How could the strapping man, who used to grab me by the belt and throw me high up in the air, be gone? But he was old, I concluded in my little six year old mind, and old people die sometimes. That's part of life.

Over the next four years, I lost two more grandparents and a great-grandparent. As a child, I continued to reason that they were old, and old people die sometimes. Only as a teenager did it dawn on me that these relatives who were so dear to me were all in their late fifties and early sixties: not young, to be sure, but definitely gone before their time.

As I approached adulthood, I noticed other little things that suggested that maybe my family's moderate indulgences were having unintended consequences. An uncle of mine required a triple bypass surgery, and another needed a quadruple bypass. Again, men I knew as strong and invincible were weakening prematurely before my eyes. What did it mean?

I should have realized that I was hardly a picture of health myself. A chronic allergy-sufferer, I was used to carrying a box of Kleenex around wherever I went. I have no childhood memories of being able to breathe through my nose, and I battled severe psoriasis. When spring came around the pollen made me miserable, and when winter came around I battled everything from bronchitis to sinus infections. Soon I was on a litany of prescription medications to manage the misery.

As an adult, I now understand the difference between being fit and being healthy. Back then I was in incredible cardiovascular shape, but I was not laying the foundation for lifelong wellness. But at 19, I still felt invincible. A year-round three-sport athlete for my entire childhood, I loved playing pick-up football and basketball in college. Just before the Christmas break, I remember hearing a pop in my knee during a tackle football game and continuing to play. After the game was over and the adrenaline wore off, I could still feel something was wrong. I walked to the infirmary, where they concluded I had probably sprained my knee. I was given a brace and crutches, but instead of using them, I simply walked home.

Only later when the leg began to swell up to three times its normal size did I realize how serious my injury was. At that point I had to be rushed to the emergency room and my walking days were over for a while. Even years later, it required surgery and physical therapy to heal completely. My "toughness" was dangerously close to recklessness. It took my brother's death, however, to make me realize that I had to do something about it.

BEYOND THE CRISIS

The Break In process is not just for times of crisis. It is a necessary and painful part of coming back from a crisis.

Once you have mastered the Break In, however, you will find it incredibly useful for optimizing performance, even when life is going well.

You go to the doctor when you are very sick, but ideally you also go to the doctor once a year for a physical, to optimize your health. In the same way, you can begin using the Break In to check on all areas of your life in order to make sure you are on track to achieve your goals.

CHAPTER FOUR: BREAKTHROUGH

We've all read books or watched movies in which a character makes a dramatic transformation: the alcoholic who pours out all his booze, the drug addict who flushes his stash, or the even the nerdy girl who gets a makeover and is crowned prom queen. Perhaps you, or someone you know, has been to a personal development seminar where everyone was hypnotized, walked on glass or fire, or had some other radically crazy experience. And the key, of course, is that after taking these radical steps, they were able to live radically different lives.

Scriptwriters and motivational speakers alike

recognize that in order to have a shot at real change, you often have to do something that might seem a little extreme. You have to take action that involves your entire being: spirit, soul and body. This is because the decisions and habits that shape the course of our lives are not isolated: they are deeply interconnected. As you will see in this chapter, both Carl and I took physical steps that sparked Breakthroughs that affected our entire lives.

RUNNING FOR MY LIFE

After my initial Break In, I started running a great deal. I had always been athletic, so a couple of miles became several miles quite naturally. Initially I used my runs to think and de-stress; then I began to run so far that I would sometimes get lost. You can only imagine the looks I got when—in full running gear—I would ask someone for directions at midnight. My stress management eventually developed into serious training, and I was honored to compete in the world-renowned 24 Hour Run US National Competition: a two mile loop that competitors run for 24 hours non-stop.

Yes, you read that correctly. We ran for 24 hours straight, and yes, it's as crazy as it sounds. Although I knew some ultra-marathoners who had completed fifty, and even one-hundred-mile races, I had never run anything close to that distance. I set three goals for myself going in: to have fun, to learn about myself, and to run at least 120 miles. Looking back, the goal of having fun was probably the most unrealistic!

But in the end, the experience was amazing. I *did* have fun, and I did learn more about myself than I could have imagined possible. Once, I found myself waking up while running: I had no idea how long I had been running asleep! For long stretches of time, I felt like I was completely alone with God, pleading with Him for the strength to keep going. I'm also pretty sure I was hallucinating between 2:00 and 4:00 AM, but when I finished I felt like a different person. I had also achieved my third goal, completing just shy of 127 miles.

Not every Breakthrough has to be an intense physical experience, but we need to experience it physically, spiritually, mentally and emotionally.

The 24-hour run was more of a mental challenge than a physical one: ultimately I learned that my mind could make my body do almost anything. But the important thing about the experience was that it showed me what was possible.

Other clients Carl has coached have had successful Breakthroughs doing other things. Some have climbed mountains; others have trained for and completed triathlons. One woman lost 80 pounds after a lifetime of being overweight. Others have found Breakthroughs through extended periods of prayer and fasting. Ultimately, the specific step you take does not matter nearly as much as its effect on you.

THE MULTI-DIMENSIONAL BREAKTHROUGH

A Breakthrough is necessary when you have to change course radically, dramatically, and in most cases, immediately. As I have already said, your Breakthrough does not have to be physical in nature. But why is it that radical changes in the way we treat our bodies, like my running, can be so successful in bringing about change in other areas of our lives? The answer lies in the fact that, whether we recognize it or not, we are deeply interconnected beings. As C.S. Lewis observed in his classic work, The Screwtape Letters, "Whatever their [humans'] bodies do affects their souls."

THE ANATOMY OF A COMEBACK

Why did the 24-hour run change me? Because it expanded (almost beyond recognition) my understanding of what was actually possible. After running 127 miles straight, I no longer wondered if the future could possibly hold anything good. I *knew* I was not a has-been, as I had secretly feared. I acquired a deep conviction that my best days were in fact before me, not behind me, as so many people had said. I had experienced a taste of the amazing things that were possible if I just focused on a goal.

I was also forced to learn a very tricky lesson about focus. It's so easy to dwell on the past or worry about the future, but during the run, I couldn't think about either. I had never been forced to focus on the smallest moment in time—over and over—for hours! I literally had no energy or attention left for boredom.

My initial strategy was to break the run down into 24 one-hour runs in my mind. But as things became more uncomfortable, I found I had to think about each hour in 5-minute segments. When the pain became even more extreme, I had to focus on getting through each minute, one at a time. By the end it was literally, "one step at a time."

My race wasn't perfect. If I let my mind wander, I felt even more exhausted thinking about the distance I had already traveled, and I began to slow down. Needless to say, if I had spent much time thinking about how much time was left, I would have stopped. So I spent hours focused on taking one more breath and one more step.

The lesson I learned was that

you can go extremely far if you just stay focused on taking your very next step.

As I began forward movement in my life, I often battled discouragement. I would be tempted to think back to the past with regret or to become overwhelmed with the distance I had to travel. But after the run, I would think back to my Breakthrough and remember: just one more breath, one more step.

Learn from the past, dream of the future, but live in the present.

Ultimately, the experience gave me the hope and motivation I needed to try again in every area of my life. If I could run 127 miles, I could succeed in business again. If I could run 127 miles, I could find love again. If I could run 127 miles, then I had really only begun to scratch the surface of what was possible in life. I could begin again, while learning from my past mistakes.

If the purpose of the Break In is to identify your current situation, the key with the Breakthrough is to shake yourself free from the assumptions and habits that got you there, or are keeping you there. I needed to shake myself free from depression, fear and hopelessness. Carl needed to be free from illness and grief. What do you need to shake yourself free from?

CARL'S BREAKTHROUGH

After a year of being depressed over the loss of my brother, I began to take stock of myself. I realized that my problem wasn't an overwhelming addiction or a major disability. I was simply living recklessly and not to my potential. My brother may have been reckless, but he didn't live a small life. He—like other members of my family—seemed to me to be absolutely fearless, "What's the worst that could happen?" was his famous catchphrase. That was what I loved most about him, and really about my entire family.

Of course with some things in life, "the worst that can happen" is that you wrap your car around a telephone pole. But I realized I had allowed that tragedy to suck the life out of everything I was doing. Jon had taken things too far, but he had at least died *living* his life. I felt dead in the wake of his death, and I knew that wasn't what he wanted.

I wanted to recapture Jon's fearlessness, but without the excesses that had ended the lives of so many I cared about. Shortly after the funeral, I attended a personal development seminar which happened to devote an entire day to wellness and nutrition. The speaker discussed, among other things, the environmental and dietary factors that contribute to allergies and general wellness. She made a lot of sense, and I was intrigued.

THE ANATOMY OF A COMEBACK

One of the exercises in the seminar was to write down everything we had eaten in the last 48 hours. I had never really critically examined what I put into my body—what teenager does?—but I found that my list contained very few foods I was proud of. After all, I was the guy who lived on McDonalds cheeseburgers and ate steak every chance I got.

So my list wasn't exactly a picture of health—but it was an honest representation of the way I was living. I waited in line to talk to the speaker one-on-one. I told her about my allergies and the medications I was on. She listened and examined my list. She circled some foods and crossed out others.

Finally, she said, "Carl, I'm not a doctor. But I want you to avoid the foods I've crossed out for thirty days, and eat only the ones I've circled."

"Okay," I said with hesitation, not sure how I was going to live without my McDonalds cheeseburgers.

"And another thing," she added. "I want you to stop taking your allergy medicines for the same period of time."

"Wow," I responded thinking this may be reckless advice coming from a non-medic. It was spring, and I was going to be working outside in my business. How was I going to survive without my medications and weekly allergy shots?

"Just give it thirty days. If it doesn't work, stop and go back to your meds."

It seemed fair enough. I hadn't ever met a single person who ate the way she was telling me to eat—let alone someone in my family—but I figured I could do anything for thirty days. "What's the worst that could happen?" I asked myself.

Within six days of following my new diet and tossing my medications, my allergy symptoms were completely gone. For the first time in my life, I remember breathing through my nose. Not only was I free of the itchy eyes, runny nose and general discomfort associated with my allergies, I had more energy than I ever thought possible.

My friends could not believe the new lifestyle I was leading, but they also couldn't believe I no longer needed to carry around a box of tissues, and that I was off my prescriptions. They mocked me relentlessly when we went out to eat—I was ordering salads instead of burgers and onion rings—but they couldn't argue with the results.

You might think this experience would have turned me into a nutrition guru, but what it really did was show me that dramatic, real change was possible. For so long I had assumed that the path my family members had taken—a path of moderate indulgence leading to gradually worsening health—was the only path there was. I had assumed my allergies were with me to stay. I had no idea that you could completely own your wellness, and reverse chronic conditions.

If I could take charge of something as important as my health, what else could I take charge of?

Taking charge of my health inspires me to take charge of the rest of my life: my relationships, my business, even my hobbies and leisure activities.

I was extremely fortunate to figure out how to orchestrate a Comeback at the age of 23. I sold my first business, and then proceeded to successfully grow two more by the age of 40. While I enjoyed landscaping, contracting and real estate development, I realized that my real passion lay in helping other people succeed in their lives, careers and businesses. I had been coaching part time for years, and I decided to make professional coaching my career. Since 2002, my company has mentored the launch of over 4000 businesses in 35 countries.

CHANGING THE PLOT

Remember in the last chapter when Chuck discussed those stories we tell ourselves? There are two sides to this phenomenon. On the one hand, we need to repeat the good stories—the ones full of mercy, grace, redemption and triumph. Again, God knew what He was doing when He established specific holidays to rehearse specific stories. On the other hand,

---

sometimes a bad story gets stuck in a continual loop; when that happens, we need a way to eject the disc and put in a new one.

I once knew a young lady, "Nancy," whose parents had neglected her quite severely when she was young. She didn't suffer any material lack, but instead lacked attention, love and care. The personal narrative she developed for herself was one of self-pity, and the ending of the story was always the same: she was neglected and unloved.

Nancy gravitated toward emotionally dysfunctional people who seemed willing to give her the attention she craved. Yet the narrative in her head quietly urged her to push her friends' buttons until they rejected her, thus giving her the ending she was used to. It wasn't pleasant, but it was familiar, and thus comfortable. Because she believed herself to be unlovable, she secretly assumed that every relationship was doomed to end this way.

Nancy was forced to Break In when she found herself still single on the eve of her fortieth birthday. She had dated for more than two decades and had been unable to build a meaningful relationship that lasted more than a few months. So she decided to Breakthrough. She didn't jump out of an airplane, run a marathon or go on a diet. She enrolled in her local community college and learned to speak French.

Nancy already held a master's degree and had studied Latin in college, but she had never learned a living foreign language. Learning French not only opened her eyes up to vast new swaths of history, culture, music, art and cuisine, but it also literally gave her a new way of communicating with people. She found that when she was speaking French she held her body differently, used different intonations, and related to people in a fresh new way. It was like playing a character in a movie, except that she soon found she liked the character better than her old self.

After a while, she adopted more and more of her French speaking persona in her everyday life. It was the key to her transformation. And while she is still single at the time of writing, she has built many more functional, lasting friendships.

Remember, it is not the Breakthrough activity itself that changes you: it is the fact that the activity breaks you free from your previous patterns of behavior and thought.

The Breakthrough shows you the possibility of a change in plot in the story of your life.

An interesting thing happens to people who Breakthrough and stick with the change (more on that in the next chapter!). In hindsight, they often observe that the negative thoughts and behaviors that seemed so ingrained in their lives weren't really "them." So where do those negative patterns come from? Sometimes it is the lies others have told us: that we are not valuable, or not good enough to be successful. Other times, the lies were unintentional: Nancy's parents never meant to tell her she was unlovable and unimportant, but their actions said that to Nancy every day.

The Breakthrough liberates us from these lies by elevating us above them. Finally, we can see that we were created for more than our problems and shortcomings. We do not become entirely different people; we gain a fresh perspective of ourselves and the person we were always meant to be.

FINDING THE BALANCE

Every change you make in your life doesn't have to be a major Breakthrough. Many people who begin exercise or nutrition programs, for example, find great success when making gradual, lasting changes. The purpose of the kind of Breakthrough we describe in this chapter is to get you out of your rut: to shake you to the point where you are able to see possibility, where you once only saw hopelessness.

Not everyone is having a crisis right now, but everyone can make improvements and grow.

Just as you can use the Break In to assess your situation when things are not going well, you can utilize less dramatic Breakthroughs throughout your life.

These often involve taking only a small step. Maybe you've never done anything athletic and you just want to train for a 5K run. You might want to finish your degree, join a weight loss group, take an art class or begin studying a musical instrument. There are plenty of smaller changes you can make in your life that can release creativity and excitement if you stick with them.

A radical step is almost always necessary when you are in a place of desperation. But the Breakthrough is only a step in the journey, it is not the destination. Too many people walk on hot coals, jump out of an airplane or visit Europe, only to find themselves back in the same rut a few weeks later. How can you prevent that from happening? In the next chapter, we'll talk about how to make sure your Breakthrough sticks.

CHAPTER FIVE: BREAK OUT

"A fire broke out on 53rd and Main Street around 10:00 this morning. Firefighters worked for hours to contain the blaze. Authorities say the cause was most likely…"

Every so often, the local news will report on a story like this one. By definition, the fire itself was completely unexpected, but in retrospect it can almost always be traced to a specific cause. An investigation might reveal it to be arson, faulty wiring, or a carelessly discarded cigarette. Whatever the culprit, the consuming blaze always begins with a single spark.

Think of your Breakthrough as a spark. Now what do you need for that spark to "catch" so you can

Breakout? Just as a fire needs favorable conditions such as dry air and wind in order to spread, you need to set up a support system for yourself that enables your Breakthrough to lead to a Breakout.

WHAT NOW?

Sometimes the day after you jump out of the airplane can be more challenging than the moment before you jump. Why? Because you've taken that radical step and shaken yourself free, but now you may feel like a ship that has just shed its anchor. Unless you have a strong sense of direction and a driving force pushing you towards your intended goal, you'll stay adrift on the ocean. And in reality, that is what happens to most people. They walk on hot coals, and then they have no idea what to do next. They stop with the Breakthrough and never complete their Comeback.

While the Breakthrough may feel scary, it's pretty straightforward once you have made up your mind. Running that marathon may make you extremely uncomfortable, but you know what to do. Living an entirely new way afterwards is a completely different matter.

It is crucial that you harness the momentum of your Breakthrough to get to the next step of your

Comeback by Breaking Out. Just as the world is full of people who were too scared to sign up for that triathlon, there are plenty of people who finish the race, but fail to capitalize on it.

In my experience, it is the Breakout that separates those who are serious about their Comeback from those who are not really willing to change.

There are moments during your Comeback when you will feel suspended in air, like a trapeze artist leaping from one bar to the next. Just like that acrobat, you can't seize what's in front of you before you let go of what's behind. But that time in between can feel like an eternity.

These moments will put an incredible demand on your faith. Your mind will try to convince you that this terrifying uncertainty is your destiny. I would have never survived if I hadn't trusted that God was in control of all the things I couldn't control, and that He would enable me to grab the next bar.

Today I know that there are only two times when I get upset about my life being unmanageable: when I don't get my way, and when I do. It's when I submit to God's will for my life, that I find peace, and things are good.

After my Breakthrough, I created a poster with some inspirational and deeply meaningful quotes. At the bottom was the Bible verse I kept at the center of my Comeback—Romans 8:28: *"We know that in all things God works for the good of those who love Him, who've been called according to His purpose."*

This reminded me that although not all things are good, God can make anything work for good. This helped me to understand that even my past mistakes could be turned around for something valuable. I resisted the urge to dwell on my past, or to feel discouraged about my present. I began to hope in my future! Even better, I began to realize that my past could not only be turned around to benefit me and my family, but also to benefit others.

We must resist the temptation to focus on ourselves so much that we miss the opportunity to bless others. A dear friend of mine struggled with a period of addiction that cost him his family, his health, and ultimately his self-respect. As he struggled to turn things around, it wasn't the addiction that held him back as much as the shame over his past.

All this changed when he was given the opportunity to help a fellow addict. Suddenly he saw his past in a redemptive light—evil being turned around for good! His terrible choices became the key to someone else's rescue. Watching his fellow man become free helped my friend to finally let go of his past and reach for the next bar.

If the key to the Breakthrough is decisive, radical action, the Breakout is all about making a plan.

Now that you see yourself and your future in a new light, take the time and effort to write down your new goals and how you will achieve them. Think of yourself as starting afresh, like a newborn baby; your future holds endless possibilities, and you are vulnerable in your new view of life. You need support, and you need to take it one step at a time. Unlike a baby, however, you have the power and wisdom available required to chart the course before you.

HOW CAN I ADD VALUE?

One of the biggest mistakes we make when we want to make a financial Comeback is to ask the question, "How can I get more money?" At first glance, this seems to be the right question. After all, the root of all financial problems is a lack of money, right?

Actually, that is not true. I had plenty of money before my crisis hit, and then all of a sudden I had less than nothing. My problem wasn't a lack of money; it was what I did with the money I had. If you think a little deeper, we all know people who have become very successful with little, and people who have got themselves deeply into debt with a lot. Clearly, there is more to a financial Comeback than just figuring out how to get more money.

Furthermore, asking "How can I get more money?" puts you in the role of a consumer or a "taker." That frame of reference ignores your role as a "producer." It implies that you are *someone who is needy rather than someone who is valuable* and therefore can provide value to others. It triggers fear, and fear never leads to good long-term decisions.

It's also worth keeping in mind that there are lots of ways to get money that don't make use of your value. After all, you can beg, borrow, steal, or try to win the lottery. So, asking how you will be able to get more money is not the right way to approach your Comeback.

The real question you need to ask yourself is (to paraphrase Author T. Harv Eker), "How can I add more value? How can I solve more problems for more people?"

This immediately puts you in the role of the provider, not taker. Jesus reminded us that we need to give in order to receive. He told His followers in Luke 6:38, "Give, and it will be given to you. A good measure, pressed down, shaken together and running over, will be poured into your lap. For with the measure you use, it will be measured to you."

Asking yourself how you can add more value triggers creativity instead of fear, and will yield many more productive answers. Ask yourself this question, and take the time to write down your answers. Those answers will be the building blocks of your Comeback plan.

When you are in a place of desperation, it may feel a little counter intuitive to focus on what you have to offer others, rather than what they can give to you. But this is absolutely crucial, whether you are an entrepreneur, an employee, or seeking employment. Stop focusing on how to find the best job or how to market yourself or your product effectively. Instead, ask yourself what need you are able to meet, what problem you are able to solve, or solve more effectively. This is an empowering thought process that leads to a focus on others and with a mindset of service. We can approach others with confidence, because we are genuinely offering something beneficial rather than simply trying to "sell."

As I was just launching my new company, I was flying across the country to meet a Fortune100 company. My business was small and funds were extremely tight. On my layover in Dallas, a bank alert notified me that payroll was processing but it was not going to clear. I jumped off the plane, took an Uber to Wells Fargo to make a funds transfer, and got back, narrowly making my next flight. Five hours later, I was presenting our solution to a multi-billion dollar company; explaining how much they needed our help. If I had focused on the fragile existence of our startup, I wouldn't have been able to "sell" anything. But, they did have a problem, and we could solve it, and that's all that mattered. We got that account and still have it to this day.

It's very important to remember that money should never be an end in itself.

Money is the natural byproduct of solving more problems.

The higher the value of the solution we provide, the more money we can expect to bring. It really is that simple.

OUT OF A JOB

At the time of writing, America has recently sustained a period with the unemployment rate in double digits. The fact is, in good times and bad, some people are working, and some aren't. There are all kinds of reasons for this, but to Break Out, we have to focus on the factors we can control. Even if you feel that losing your job was 99% downsizing, your boss's prejudice or something else that had nothing to do with you, focus on the 1% in your power. This isn't blaming yourself; it's finding the key to your Comeback!

Ask yourself if there was anything you could have done to make yourself more indispensable at your previous job. It really does not matter what line of work you are in; you can almost always take steps to make yourself more valuable to your employer.

Lewis, for example, is a maintenance man at a manufacturing plant. He got his job straight out of high school, and became one of six janitors working eight-hour shifts. After he married, Lewis knew his job security was more important than ever, so he started watching for ways to make himself more valuable. He realized that one of the most important pieces of equipment he and his coworkers were responsible for was the boiler, the large furnace that heated the facility through the cold months. He learned how disastrous a boiler failure could be by listening to the older maintenance men: pipes could freeze, other machinery could be ruined, or the operations in the factory could even be halted. Lewis decided to take extra classes to get his boiler certification, which would enable him to service and troubleshoot the boiler. (This is a prime example of using the "Break In" process without a crisis!)

Just before Lewis's first daughter was born, rumors of layoffs began circulating around the plant. Lewis and his wife crossed their fingers and waited. Two janitors were let go: one had been hired before Lewis; neither had a boiler certification. Now that the crew was down to four, instead of six, they would often work their shifts alone. When push came to shove, the management knew that Lewis was more valuable than the older man who had been there longer because he could service the boiler.

If you are currently unemployed, try to look at your situation as feedback on your performance or qualifications. As painful as it sounds, that is the only way to improve as a result of your crisis. Now you may feel that you did a good, or even a great job at your previous position, and you might be right. Nevertheless, can you honestly say there was nothing you could have done better, more effectively, more creatively or more efficiently? Perhaps you worked for a dysfunctional organization; what can you do to make your skills desirable to a healthier company?

You want to put yourself in a position so that any employer would be crazy not to hire you. To do that, put yourself in the shoes of prospective employers. What do they want? What do they need?

If you're an entrepreneur, put yourself in a position so that the prospect with the need would be crazy not to buy from you. What problem does that person really have?

Focus on solving their problem, not selling your product or service.

How can you provide a solution that is a "no-brainer"? When you start thinking in these terms, the path to your Breakout becomes much clearer.

MY BREAK OUT PLAN

After the 24-hour run, I began to give more thought to what I was most passionate about, as well as turning my attention to the business climate at the time. I began following business news more closely with that question in the back of my mind, "How can I add more value in this economy? How can I solve more problems for people right now?"

When we ask this question, we need to consider the market, as well as our passion, experience and skills. I began to notice that many smaller entrepreneurs were struggling to adjust to a world that was increasingly driven by the Internet. I realized that, even with my own struggles, I had the passion and experience to help these entrepreneurs succeed. I began to realize that my years in the business world provided a way that I could add value, but I knew I didn't have the time to be vague about it. I had to be specific, so I took the following steps:

1. Clarify

The first thing I did was to clarify the financial situation I had confronted during my Break In. It was time to get real. I had to write down all my monthly expenses, my debt as well as my income, which was very little at the time. I also took the time to clarify what I was actually working for. Although lack of money was an issue, money was no longer an end in itself. I knew that I was working because I wanted to take care of my needs, provide for my family, and help others. I also wanted to be a great example to my kids. The money itself became secondary to those goals. Once I had focused on the "why," I knew I would figure out the "how." Carl and I have found this to be true of Comebacks in general:

---

once you're connected to your purpose, the means of achieving your goals often become much clearer.

---

2. Adjust

Next, I had to adjust to my present realities. First I looked at my expenses: where could I tighten the belt? I moved into a smaller home, which immediately reduced both my monthly housing and utility bills. I drove my remaining Mercedes back to the dealership, turning it in as a voluntary repossession. To replace it,

I bought a used Dodge Caravan. I also looked at all my other expenses, including food and clothing, to see where I could save money.

Of course this adjustment was painful.

Many people see a reduction in their material goods as a "setback," but I knew my adjustments were actually a step forward in my Comeback.

I realized that the piles of possessions I accumulated before actually made me vulnerable to the kind of crisis I endured. I didn't want them anymore. I wanted to come back to complete financial freedom, and I saw this as an empowering step in that direction.

Another mistake I've seen people make at this stage of the Comeback process is to assume that they are in so much financial trouble that trimming their grocery bill won't make a difference. While it's true that saving fifty dollars a week on food or other items won't prevent a foreclosure, it *can* allow you to pay down a credit card. The larger principle at work is learning the self-discipline to live within your means. Even small exercises in self-control, such as resisting carry out for dinner one night and making a sandwich instead, or passing on new clothes and making what you have work, will move you on the path to freedom. Do it with the mindset of forward progress.

3. Assess

My next step was to assess the gap between my income and expenses for my (and my family's) basic needs. Some may find that by drastically reducing their expenses, they are able to live within their reliable income. Due to the fact that I had virtually no income, I found that I was still coming up very short. I would need to take immediate steps to increase my income. Whatever your assessment shows, the key is to determine that you will not stay at the survival level for long.

During this time I learned how little I needed in life to be happy. I certainly enjoy nice things as much as the next person, but

I realized during my Comeback that happiness is much more about enjoying the moments, than the things.

I experienced incredible enjoyment creating a makeshift golf course on our backyard greenbelt with my boys, having a walk by the lake with my wife and our kids, or renting a movie and making popcorn, compared to simply going to fancy restaurants or out to the theater.

It was actually refreshing to be creative about family time and entertainment, rather than feeling obliged to go to the "best" amusement park or on the "best" vacation. The simple pleasures in life offered us far more quality time, and strengthened our relationships. We appreciated everything more, and experienced the joy more deeply. This also proved great practice for maintaining a better balance in my expenditures once I was financially back on my feet.

4. Plan According to Passion and Purpose

Now I had to figure out how to make up the gap. Because a Comeback takes a phenomenal amount of energy,

---

it is best to pour that energy into something that not only has income potential, but also involves what we are passionate about.

There are really two main questions I asked myself in this stage:

1. What *can* I do?
2. What do I *want* to do?

I had been in marketing for years; that is what I knew *how* to do. I had studied marketing, taught marketing and built marketing teams over the years that generated millions of dollars in revenue. I wanted to get into Internet marketing, which was really a way of updating the skill set I already had in order to serve a new generation of entrepreneurs. The questions I asked: Could I become successful at it fast enough to make up the gap in my income and expenses? Ideally, could I become successful enough at it to become financially free? Was I passionate enough about it to pay the price?

My wife Wendy is very fond of telling me to "Go big or go home!" I knew I'd go big, but I needed to start from the beginning. It was time to count the cost (in time, money and energy) of updating my skills. I had a college degree in computer science and had built a few websites, but that was almost 20 years ago. Twenty years in the computer world is forever. I checked into various universities that offered the training I needed, but they were expensive and wouldn't allow me to keep working during the day easily. So instead I searched for a mentor. I found several top Internet marketers and decided to borrow, in order to invest sacrificially in their coaching and training programs. I did almost all of my training at home by staying up late into the night and getting up extra early.

If my schedule sounds crazy, it's because it was. It was an insane amount of work, but it had a purpose. I looked at it as doing what I had to do. I have friends who worked 120 hours a week as medical interns or stayed up for weeks at a time studying for the bar exam. Future doctors and lawyers do this, not because this is the pace they intend to keep up for the rest of their lives, but because they know their career requires this kind of initial investment of massive amounts of time and energy.

I knew where I was going with my plan, and I committed to it with everything I had. I took the momentum from the 24-hour run and poured that enthusiasm into this new business. I was bound—and determined—to make it happen!

FINDING REAL PURPOSE

We've all heard wonderful exhortations to "do what you love," but in truth, it may be an extensive journey to arrive at that reality. Pursuing what we think we would love to do is good, but it can be irresponsible if it is not compatible with our current level of skill, or our realistic current opportunities. There may first be a price to pay, and timing to acknowledge. And it's worth noting that all work involves activities we don't naturally love.

THE ANATOMY OF A COMEBACK

So learning to apply positive meaning to the work that we do, is just as important as pursuing what we love.

I'll take it one step further: finding real purpose does not come from simply doing what we love or assigning positive meaning to our work; real purpose comes from considering doing what will help us become the person we'd like to be. Real purpose is found both in the impact your work has on others as well as on yourself. Now, if you're deep in survival mode gasping for air, then even attempting to think about who you'd like to become may be a challenge. But push your thinking: Considering what you can do, and what you want to do, what would success look like? And who would you become in that process? Those answers will tell you a lot.

So what if you don't like your job, but you still need it? Many people do work they aren't particularly passionate about because they are good at it, or because it is the job available to them. One woman I knew was a highly skilled attorney for a large automobile corporation. She did not particularly enjoy her job, but she needed to keep it until her husband finished his Ph.D. When she was staying up late preparing for a trial, she chose to focus on their two daughters, and on their family's future. That gave her the motivation to continue to excel in her job. She was able to find joy in what her job did for her family, even though the day-to-day process was often frustrating. The result was not only an ability to perform well and feel great value from her work, but she developed her character as a selfless, giving individual.

Throughout human history, people have labored to feed, clothe and shelter themselves. We are extremely blessed to live in an era in which we can often do much better than that. We will not always be "doing what we love," but we can always love the reasons we do it.

SAME JOB, NEW APPROACH

One of Carl's clients, Mike, faced a financial crisis when he got upside down in some real estate investments. Not yet thirty, he was forced to declare bankruptcy and start over. After assessing his situation, Mike traded in his convertible and moved into a friend's basement apartment. He continued his regular job as a sales representative for a food grower, traveling to various markets to persuade them to carry his employer's products.

When real estate was hot, Mike had treated sales as his day job, focusing his energy on his other investments. After facing the reality of his bankruptcy, he started to think of ways he could get more out of the reliable job that he had. He began to pay attention to the conversations he was having with store owners, buyers and other distributors that purchased his products. He noted things such as their hobbies and family interests: who liked fishing and whose kid had just won the state championship tennis match.

Mike started moving beyond doing his job to building meaningful relationships with his customers; he enjoyed his job more and his employer soon realized he was becoming a highly effective ambassador for the company. The company was expanding, partially due to Mike's success, and his boss soon granted him a larger territory. This came with a higher salary, a larger expense budget, a company car and full medical benefits. He was soon able to move to a larger place and build up his savings again, simply by making the extra effort to learn more about his customer.

Charlene, on the other hand, was a third grade teacher. She was engaged to be married at the time she chose her career, thinking that it would be a supplemental, rather than the primary income for their household. When her fiancé dumped her unexpectedly, she realized that she not only had to rethink her personal plans, but her financial plans as well. She took stock of her situation, and noted that her work responsibilities, as well as salary and benefits were well defined. Her job, however, did not financially reward her in direct proportion to her performance. She knew for a fact that her students had performed better on the school's standardized tests than the four other classes in the school, but as satisfying as this was, she wouldn't get any extra money.

After careful consideration, Charlene decided to pursue a master's in teaching, helping her rise on the pay scale. Although she was accepted to some prestigious schools, she opted to do her graduate school work at her local community college, to avoid incurring any debt. To improve her financial situation in the short term, she began tutoring during the summer and coaching the girls' volleyball team. Charlene's unexpected relationship change sparked a Comeback in her career!

CARL: LEARNING FROM A MASTER

Years ago, I (Carl) was at a fitness conference, and in one of the afternoon sessions, the trainer was delayed. This kind of thing can really get on your nerves, because you've paid all this money, traveled to an event, and you want to make sure you're getting the maximum possible value for your trouble. The attendees were just starting to get restless when we learned that someone else had volunteered to lead our class, and that someone was none other than Stu Mittleman, the ultra-distance world champion and world record holder!

Stu greeted our class and right away volunteered to take us on a run. Talk about your dream come true! There was only one little problem: the original class was supposed to be only theoretical instruction, not activity, so I had left my running shoes in my hotel room. In fact, I was wearing glorified moccasins with no socks! But the group was leaving right away. I knew I couldn't pass up the opportunity, so I ran barefoot with Stu Mittleman for an hour, carrying my shoes in my hand!

So why did I willingly allow my feet to bleed for a week? Because Stu had mastered the sport that I was just beginning. He had the level of health and fitness that I wanted. And with my feet throbbing the entire way, I absorbed every word he said. "Hold your hands like you're cradling two butterflies. Don't grab too hard. You'll crush the butterflies and chew up too much energy. Run in the middle of the road because it's flat. If you run on either side, the slope will throw your hips out of balance. Run so you can breathe comfortably and talk to the person next to you. If you can't talk to the person next to you, you're running too hard."

Not long after, I ran the New York City Marathon. I followed every bit of Stu's advice: cradling my butterflies in the middle of the road without running too hard. Before that day, I hadn't run more than ten miles in my life. Yet I was able to run the entire race, start to finish.

THE ANATOMY OF A COMEBACK

When you Break Out, you are doing something you've never done before.

In addition to creating that master plan, you need to seek out people who have already accomplished what you want to accomplish. Find a way to learn from them, as I did with Stu, or as Chuck did with the Internet marketing experts. These are the kind of people who will be able to lead you towards your intended destination. Their wisdom will allow you to grow much faster than if you were left to learn only on your own.

Now in addition to people leading you, you're going to need others by your side. It would have been great to have Stu Mittleman as my daily running partner, but he was a little busy to work me into his schedule. So you need some folks that may not be exactly where you want to be themselves, but they're headed in the same direction. We'll talk about that more in the next chapter.

The early days with my boys

Through the journey together

THE ANATOMY OF A COMEBACK

Our crazy family

Our little princess

Father's Day

Our family today

THE ANATOMY OF A COMEBACK

Me and my dog

CHAPTER SIX: BREAK AWAY

So here we are. We've broken in, taking inventory of our current situation and how we got here. We've Broken Through, taking that radical step that shakes us out of our rut and reminds us what is possible. And we've Broken Out, making that master plan and establishing a foundation for a new life. Now it's time to put feet to that plan. It's time to Break Away.

NEW HABITS

When Steven Covey released the Seven Habits of Highly Effective People in 1989, he revolutionized the world of personal development for countless individuals. The book popularized the idea that one's outlook on life and cultivated behaviors were far more powerful in shaping one's outcomes than various isolated decisions.

Indeed it is our habits that enable us to break away.

Developing new habits is vital to your Breakaway for several reasons. Naturally, a crisis or a setback can cause anyone a great deal of anxiety; if you're not careful, this can undermine your goals. At various points in my own Comeback process, I struggled to sleep well, and found myself unfocused and lethargic during the day. Of course running became a great way to manage my stress, but I also found that by establishing new habits, I was able to better channel my energy productively.

A good daily routine can be comforting, especially at a time in your life when everything else feels a bit unpredictable. Enriching habits not only help you to stay focused and make the most of your time, they also prevent stress from distracting you. As you put feet to your master plan, try to identify some new practices to incorporate into your schedule; start with a time of quiet meditation or prayer at the beginning of each day. Try regular exercise or meet with a group of encouraging people. Soon you'll discover more activities that enhance your life in various ways.

Habits shape our character and what we get out of life far more than natural ability or talent. You can be a child prodigy with bad habits, and you will probably end up dealing with a lot of frustration and failure. On the other hand,

---

someone of unremarkable talent and intelligence can achieve tremendous success with the right set of habits.

Think of your habits as the current in a stream. It is much easier to swim with the current than against it, so if your habits are pushing you in the direction you want to go, you'll get there faster and with far less effort. The chances are, however, if you are in need of a Comeback, you have a few habits that are pushing you away from where you want to be. This means that you'll be swimming against the current, making progress slower, and getting tired much faster.

I realized that my old investing habits and work habits played a huge role in getting me into trouble in the first place. Turning those around was key to breaking away. What about you? Taking into account the strengths and weaknesses that you assessed in your Break In, write down a list of old habits you need to get rid of and new habits you need to cultivate. What habits led to your break down? What new habits will prevent you from making those same mistakes again? Think of it as setting up a support system for your Break Out plan, to ensure that you'll still be following it in six months or 10 years.

Part of your Breakout will be learning to make the same 24 hours of the day more productive than they ever were for you in the past. Carl found particular success utilizing the recurring appointments feature on his smartphone to make sure that all the habits he valued made their way into his life. Some of our clients have benefitted from wakeup calls, workout buddies, and accountability partners. If you spend much of your day at your desk, you may find a timer on your screen or a reminder mobile app helpful. You will need to find a tool to help you stay focused and on track as you navigate this major shift in your life.

Remember to schedule time for personal enrichment and spiritual nourishment as well. Mounting a Comeback and then sustaining it will tax you both physically and emotionally. It can be one of the toughest times of your life, as well as one of the most rewarding. Now, more than ever, it's important to ask yourself where you draw your strength and inspiration. I drew mine from my faith, my family and my church community. Before my crisis, I had found myself drifting away from investing in those relationships. During my Comeback, I made sure I re-established the habits of spending quality time with the people who mattered most to me.

RENEWING YOUR MIND

In the case of your Breakaway, it means changing the way you think about money, and the way you think about work.

Any lasting transformation involves changing the way we think.

During my own Breakaway, I realized that I was an unhealthy optimist, thinking the recurring income I had created was forever. That thinking set me up for the fall. As John Maxwell says, "The pessimist complains about the wind. The optimist expects it to change. The leader adjusts the sails." For me, I wasn't the optimist in a bad situation thinking it would change to good, but, instead, I was in a good place thinking it could never go bad. Either way, it was time to grow into a bigger leader.

The best way to combat an incorrect view is to cultivate its opposite. During my breakaway, I practiced self-restraint with my spending, as well as focusing on God, my wife and children and other important relationships as my real source of joy and encouragement. Some of my friends grew up with a deep jealousy of friends who had more money or possessions than they did. Even as adults, they struggled with feelings of lack when they saw others with nicer cars, bigger houses or more expensive vacations. To be free from this attitude, cultivate a sense of gratitude for what you do have. Spend time helping people less fortunate than you, volunteering for a job training program or a homeless shelter. These kinds of experiences—again putting yourself in the position of a giver—will help keep your own struggles in perspective, and help you not to misuse money.

Other people struggle with believing that being rich or having financial abundance makes someone "bad." They believe that you cannot become wealthy without taking from others, rather than understanding that the more people you are able to serve, the greater your income will typically become. Such folks will many times unknowingly sabotage their own success: they may shy away from pursuing a promotion at work, getting that extra certification, and so on, because they believe those kinds of efforts make them selfish or overly ambitious. If you struggle with this attitude, focus on how financial abundance allows you to bless others, and to spend more time with your family, or to invest in other relationships. Rather than earning just enough to cover your basic expenses, you can earn enough to make a difference in the lives of others!

Many of us also need to rethink our view of work. Some of us see work solely as a way of getting money, rather than a way to contribute to a company or a community and to use our God-given abilities. When times get tough, business owners may feel the world is against them, and employees may feel taken for granted. The best strategy during your Breakaway is to put yourself in other people's shoes: how do you think your boss is feeling right now? The chances are, he or she would love to see you as a cash-generating asset rather than a cash-draining liability. Are you a vital part of the team, or are you just doing the bare minimum?

DO WHAT IT TAKES

In order to Break Away, you need to be willing to do what others are not doing. For me, that meant staying up late and stretching myself to learn things that others weren't willing to learn. For a friend of mine, Charlie, it meant taking a second job for a short season just to get his family out of debt. His wife was home with the three little girls, when their only car needed an expensive repair. They were barely making ends meet and did not have the money to fix the car. They put it on the credit card, but rather than pay the interest every month, Charlie worked the early morning shift at the local McDonalds for two months in addition to his regular job. This kept them from falling behind, allowed them to build up some emergency savings, and enabled his wife to continue to take care of their children.

Kyle needed some startup capital for a breakaway business idea, so for two years, instead of taking his two weeks of paid vacation from his regular job, he did part-time labor work for a local construction company. Not only did he save the money he would have spent on a vacation, he collected his regular salary and earned extra money. It was a sacrifice, but he launched his business debt-free.

The bad news is there is no easy trick to Breaking Away. The good news is that once you've Broken Away, you will find that your new life will feel just as natural as your old life once did. We all know that it takes a lot more energy to get an airplane off the ground than it does to keep it in the air. Once the euphoria of your Breakthrough wears off, you may find yourself fatigued, and perhaps even discouraged. That's okay.

All the stuff you learned in your Break In is still true: you are still in your current situation. Some people think that having faith means that your situation will somehow magically change. And in a few rare cases, this may be true. But most often, we need to apply our faith in two specific ways: we need to trust that God will work in us to rise to the occasion, and we need to trust that our Comeback will be worth the price.

HUMBLE ENOUGH TO SUCCEED

We've all heard the saying that pride comes before a fall. The reverse is also true: humility often comes before success. One of my mentors had a favorite saying:

"Don't let your ego get in the way of your economics."

The sad reality is that many people stay in terrible financial situations because they are too proud to do particular types of work. Perhaps they have advanced to a managerial position, and they consider reporting to someone else to be moving backward. Perhaps they've never had a blue collar job in their lives and they feel they are "above" that type of work.

The simple fact is, that if you are taking your Comeback seriously, then you should not be "above" any measure to move toward your goals. Charlie had been a successful salesman for many years. Things got tight when a downturn in his industry coincided with the birth of their third child. But he didn't view his time at McDonalds as a step back. He saw it as a step toward his goals for his family.

You should never think of any step in your Comeback plan as moving backward, even if you need to take a job that seems to be at a lower level than ones you have had before. Any job is a step forward from no job at all, just as any income is a step up from no income. Starting a business means you do it all in the beginning. Remember, it is your goals and your plan that make your steps meaningful. You could be a high level manager spending all your money, and you are basically headed nowhere. On the other hand, 90% of Domino's Pizza franchise owners started out delivering pizza. So any given pizza deliveryman might retire ahead of a manager; it all depends on their plan, and what they do with their money.

CHOOSE YOUR FRIENDS WISELY

You've probably heard the saying that you're the sum of the five people you hang around the most. What does this really mean? It means people who hang out with unhealthy people are typically unhealthy, and people who hang out with athletic folks are typically athletic. If your five closest friends are broke, the chances are you are too. If the five people you talk to most often on the phone watch a lot of television, it is unlikely that you spend your free time visiting museums or going to the symphony.

There are both biological and cultural reasons for this. Our brains are designed from birth to mimic those around us: this is how we learn to speak, walk and feed ourselves. On a social level, we all want to fit in. We find it comforting to behave similarly to those around us.

When it comes to your Comeback, you need to do two things: you need to critically evaluate your relationships, and think about how to establish some new ones. Now this idea often causes confusion for many folks. They think I'm asking them to stop talking to their cousin, ditch their best friend from high school, or even worse, distance themselves from their spouse. I'm saying nothing of the sort. Any truly successful person is, by definition, completely committed to his or her family. And there is no reason you cannot move forward with your Comeback plan while staying true to friends that you have had throughout your journey.

You need to evaluate whether or not the dynamic of certain relationships is encouraging you in the wrong direction, or even weighing you down.

This is easy to understand when you consider the struggles of a recovering alcoholic. He can stay friends with his old drinking buddies, but he can't go out with them on Friday nights anymore.

But what about people who are recovering from a financial crisis? They need to be alert to those whose company brings out their weaker tendencies. Maybe they're people who just spend the evening wasting time, talking about things that really don't matter. Others love to talk about their problems, but if you take a step back, you realize they are talking about the same problems over and over. If you are spending most of your free time around people who are not at a place in life that you want to be (or at least headed reliably in that direction) then you need to re-evaluate those relationships.

Just like your habits, the company you keep nudges and encourages you in a particular direction;

---

make sure your friends are pushing you where you want to go.

A key part of Breaking Away is finding ways to spend time around people who inspire and challenge you to do your best, and to be at your best. In addition to my incredibly supportive parents and wife, I sought out specific mentors in the Internet marketing world, as I mentioned in the last chapter. But I also engaged my co-author Carl's advice and accountability for the growth of my overall business. For my personal life, as well as for my business, I gained immeasurable wisdom from Dr. Wes Beavis. He is not only a brilliant author, speaker and entrepreneur, but also a tremendous family man with degrees in theology and psychology. When I started my new company, I chose to launch it with Robert Clark because he's not only an extremely smart internet marketer, but has tremendous ethics and is someone I knew I could trust. And, finally, as I grew my new company, I made sure that my new employees could contribute not only a specific skill, but also to an uplifting culture. I also looked for investors who could not only contribute capital, but also provide additional value towards the company's success—which is why I'm so grateful for my key investors Ted Verdon, Doug Sinclair and Valerie Syme. They are all extremely smart and deeply caring people. It's about surrounding yourself with the right people.

And it isn't only who you spend time with physically. You choose who you talk to on your commute, whether it's on the phone or in a carpool. The time to and from work can be exceptionally valuable. Are you just passing the time, or are you making the most of it? How many powerful books on Audible could you listen to each month during that time? Focus on constantly learning, growing and being dialed in.

Part of Breaking Away is ensuring that you are bombarding yourself with positive input

---

that will challenge and encourage you to see your plan all the way through.

FROM CARL: THINKING BIG

The group of people I (Carl) have chosen to invest my time with has helped me to levels of success I would never have achieved otherwise. My wife in particular likes to think big. She lives in the world of "both/and" and not "either/or." She was taught as a child that if you can't decide between two options, you should take both. I've noticed that the longer we've been together, the bigger I think! This has really helped me Break Away in my decision making, to a point where I can now discern options that I would never have even imagined before I met her.

In a recent business meeting, a strategic business partner made me a very lucrative offer to run a substantial division of his business. Unfortunately, the deal required me to relocate to another part of the country. That would have meant uprooting my family, which I wasn't willing to do. Instead of turning down the offer, however, I followed my wife's lead and counter-offered. The result? I oversee and advise that division of their company as an independent contractor: both/and, not either/or! I wouldn't have thought of this option on my own, but with her encouragement, we got the best outcome possible for everyone concerned.

WHO'S THE BOSS?

Business owners love being their own bosses, but that freedom comes with tremendous responsibility.

Regar•less of whether you are an employee or an entrepreneur, everyone is the boss of his or her own Comeback.

The process rests on you and your ability to fulfill your responsibilities, even when no one is looking over your shoulder.

THE ANATOMY OF A COMEBACK

Even your accountability partners can't manage your Comeback for you. I have met some people who think that signing up for mentorship means that it's their mentor's responsibility to make sure they become successful. In reality, a mentor just offers guidance, wisdom and accountability. No one will make you Break Away except you. The Book of Proverbs explains it this way:

Go to the ant, you sluggard; consider its ways and be wise! It has no commander, no overseer or ruler, yet it stores its provisions in summer and gathers its food at harvest. How long will you lie there, you sluggard? When will you get up from your sleep? A little sleep, a little slumber, a little folding of the hands to rest—and poverty will come on you like a bandit and scarcity like an armed man.

(Proverbs 6:6-11)

One of Carl's coaching clients, Laura, finally Broke Away when she decided to take ownership of her own professional life. Laura was deeply frustrated with a certification company that had promised her support for her struggling consulting practice. Carl challenged her to turn the frustration into her own business. Under Carl's guidance, she listed the services she needed for her practice that were not provided. Then he helped her make a business plan and create an advisory board filled with top industry professionals. The board then helped her with start-up capital and structural guidance.

She convenes quarterly meetings with her advisory board, which includes Carl, so they can discuss her strategic growth, manage cash flow and minimize expenses. Her Breakaway took her from a struggling consultant to an industry leader!

LEARN TO ENJOY THE RIDE

Your Comeback is a process more than a destination, because everyone can always find some way to improve, no matter how much they achieve. In fact, I would go so far as to say that the process IS the destination. And, the *true* value is in the person we BECOME during the journey. So, embrace and enjoy your journey!

My parents taught me long ago that part of maturity is doing things you don't want to. However, if we view the hard work that we have to invest in our Comeback as mere drudgery, we will burn out quickly. We need to be careful to keep the big picture in mind, especially when we're exhausted from working a late night, or frustrated with doing something we don't care for.

Ultimately, we are responsible for the meaning we assign to our work, whatever it may be. No one enjoys cleaning up the juice that our children spill, but some look at it as drudgery due to the effort involved, while others associate it with the blessing of having children. In the same way, the long hours and sacrifices do not have to be isolated sufferings: they can be part of your journey to financial freedom. For me, much of the fuel of my Comeback came from wanting to be a successful example to my kids.

I didn't want them growing up to see a father who was knocked down and never got up.

Instead, I was driven to show them how, when life delivers a blow that flattens you to the ground, you can regroup, grow, and Come back.

After the Superbowl, or the NBA championships or the Olympics, athletes almost always reflect on all the hard work they put in to get to that moment of victory. The hard work you put into your Comeback can be the same way: it can be effort that will make your ultimate achievements all the sweeter.

The better your attitude about your actions, the more likely you are to be promoted, or to have doors opened. As Paul said, "*Whatever you do, work at it with all your heart, as working for the Lord, not for human masters*" (Colossians 3:23). It is easy to think that some people are just "lucky," and certainly some people are given opportunities they did not earn. This may be because of the people they know, family connections or other advantages. It makes no sense, however, to focus on things you cannot control. You have 100% control over your own attitude and the meaning you assign the events in your life. The more you choose a positive attitude and a productive outlook, the more you may find yourself making your own "luck."

Anyone can be "happy" when life is going well. During your Comeback, you should find the joy that does not depend on circumstances or particular outcomes. As long as you believe that you must be able to have this or obtain that in order to be joyful, you will focus on what you don't have. Again, Paul offered wisdom, "*I know what it is to be in need, and I know what it is to have plenty. I have learned the secret of being content in any and every situation*" (Philippians 4:12).

When you learn to focus on being grateful for what you have, you will be able put passion into whatever you do. There is certainly nothing wrong with looking forward to a more comfortable future, but we can never allow that to steal our joy from right now.

CONCLUSION

Wherever you are in the Comeback process right now, remember that there is something greater at work. There was a reason I rose to the heights I did, fell as far as I did, and was able to come back stronger than ever. The most painful times I endured paved the way for the most joyful times. Our Breakdown is often the result of our poor decision making as well as of events beyond our control. But in the grand scheme of things, the entire Comeback process is the way God builds character in us; it is what makes us the individuals we are. The greater purpose at work is not always obvious, but one day it will all be clear.

Carl often asks his clients to identify the highest and lowest points of their lives and place them on a timeline. The high points range from promotions to tremendous achievements, and wonderful family moments. The low points could be tough times or even horrific tragedies. In retrospect, they realize that tough times test us, stretch us, and help us to build our strength and stamina for the next chapter in our lives.

We hope this peek inside the anatomy of a Comeback gives you are more accurate picture of what it takes to go from Breakdown to a triumph that is both complete and sustainable. If you are in need of any further resources to support your efforts, we are here to help you every step of the way. Whatever comes, know that your life, your family, and your Comeback is worth everything you invest in it!

Break Away…and Godspeed

EPILOGUE

The only way to describe my life right now is to say that I am truly blessed. While no one's Comeback journey is ever truly complete, I have made more progress than I could have ever dreamed possible.

My family is thriving. My boys are growing up to be amazing young men, and I'm remarried to a beautiful Godly woman with whom I have a very spunky little girl. I co-founded and run a social technology company, Rallio, which helps national multi-location brands build online communities, manage their social media and online reputation at the local level, and drive sales.

Of course, the entire Comeback process tested my faith. Through it, I grew much closer to God, learning to lean on Him rather than on myself. I found that the more I focused on Him, the more I realized that His will for my life is so much better than anything I could come up with on my own and, simply, that everything would be alright.

Ultimately, as we've emphasized throughout the book, a Comeback is a life journey. It's about so much more than money. Your business, your career, and your personal finances are simply one measure of how you handle what has been entrusted to you. The amount you have earned, saved, given and spent is just a scorecard in the game. We wrote *The Anatomy of a Comeback* to show you how, even after a huge setback, you can still win.

Made in the USA
Columbia, SC
21 June 2018